ESTATE PUBLICATIONS

BARNSTAPLE · BIDEFORD
BRAUNTON · ILFRACOMBE · GREAT TORRINGT

G000162509

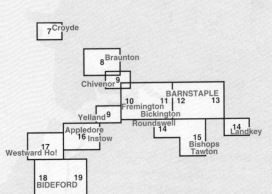

4 Ilfracombe

5

Woolacombe 7

7 Croyde

8 Braunton

Chivenor 9

BARNSTAPLE

10 11 | 12 13

Fremington
Bickington
Roundswell

Yelland 9

14

14 Landkey

Appledore
16 Instow

15 Bishops Tawton

17 Westward Ho!

18 19 BIDEFORD

20 Great Torrington

ROAD MAP .... Page 2
BARNSTAPLE ENLARGED CENTRE ... Page 3
INDEX TO STREETS .... Page 21

Scale of street plans: 4 Inches to 1 Mile (unless otherwise stated)

Motorway	Every effort has been made to verify the accuracy of information in this book but the publishers cannot accept responsibility for expense or loss caused by an error or omission. Information that will be of assistance to the user of the maps will be welcomed. The representation on these maps of a road, track or path is no evidence of the existence of a right of way.	 Stream / River
'A' Road / Dual		 Canal
'B' Road / Dual		→ One-way Street
Minor Road / Dual		P Car Park
Track		C Public Convenience
Pedestrianized		i Tourist Information
Railway / Station		+ Place of Worship
Footpath		● Post Office

Street plans prepared and published by ESTATE PUBLICATIONS, Bridewell House, TENTERDEN, KENT.
The Publishers acknowledge the co-operation of the local authorities
of towns represented in this atlas.

Ordnance Survey® This product includes mapping data licensed from Ordnance Survey®
with the permission of the Controller of Her Majesty's Stationery Office.

BRISTOL
CHANNEL

BARNSTAPLE
or
BIDEFORD BAY

Bull Pt.
Morte Pt.
Woolacombe
Morte Bay
Baggy Pt.

Ilfracombe
Lee
Mortehoe
Slade
B3343
Trimstone
West Down
Pickwell
North Buckland
Georgeham
Croyde
B3231
Saunton
Knowle
Halsinger
Braunton
Braunton Burrows
Heaton Punchardon
Wrafton
Chivenor
R. Taw
Fremington
Yelland
Appledore
Westward Ho!
Instow
Northam
Abbotsham
Bickleton
Westleigh
Bideford
East-the-Water
Horns Cross
Fairy Cross
Littleham
Landcross
Weare Giffard
Parkham
Buckland Brewer
Monkleigh
Great Torrington
Frithelstock
Haytown
Bulkworthy
Stibb Cross
Langtree
Little Torrington
Peters Marland
Abbots Kington
Newton
Winswell

Combe Martin Bay
Hele
Combe Martin
Berrynarbor
A399
Heale
Kentisbury
Patchole
Black Ga
Bittadon
East Down
Arlington
Wistlandpoun Resr.
B3230
A3123
A361
Milltown
A39
Muddiford
Loxhore
Knightacott
Marwood
Shirwell
Bratton Fleming
Pippacott
Prixford
Ashford
Goodleigh
Stoke Rivers
Barnstaple
Gunn
Bickington
Roundswell
Landkey
West Buckland
A39
Tawstock
Bishop's Tawton
A361
Swimbridge
Horwood
Newton Tracey
Ensis
Herner
Cobbaton
Chapelton
Chittlehampton
Woodtown
B3232
Hiscott
Alverdiscott
A377
Yarnscombe
Atherington
Umberleigh
B3227
Warkleigh
B3227
Sherwood Green
High Bickington
R. Tow
Chittlehamholt
St. Giles in the Wood
Kingscott
Roborough
B3217
Burrington
B3227
A386
Beaford
A3124
Riddlecombe
Ashreigney
Dolton

Marti

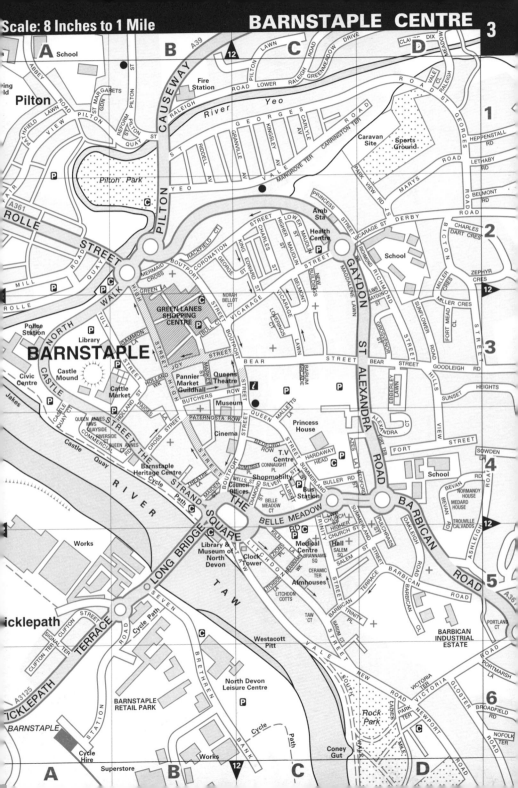

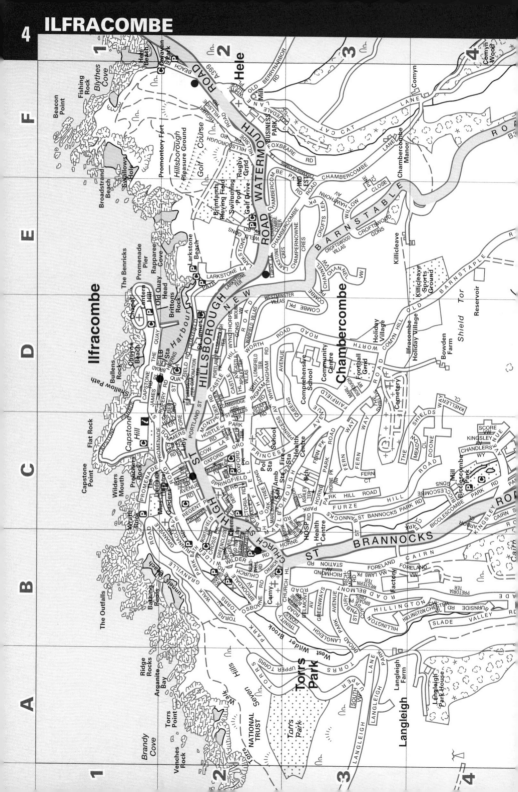

Iron Letters Cross

Two Pots

Warmscombe Wood

Warmscombe

Francis Plantation

Francis

Two Pots Farm

Sewage Works

Oakridge

Oakridge Plantation

Shelfin Hill

Great Shelfin Farm

Winsham Farm

Winsham Wood

Cleave Wood

Scorr Valley Country House

The Cairn Nature Reserve

Shelfin Wood

Shelfin Cleave

Mullacott Cleave

MULLACOTT CROSS INDUSTRIAL ESTATE

Shire Horse Centre

Mullacott Farm

Lower Slade

Lower Mullacott

Higher Mullacott

Mullacott Cross

Mullacott Cross Caravan Park

Lower Reservoir

Little Shelfin Farm

BARNSTABLE ROAD

ROAD

VALLEY ROAD

SALTMER CLOSE

SLADE

DOGGIE LANE

B3230

A3123

A361

B3343

5 6 7 8

A B C D E F

Combe Martin

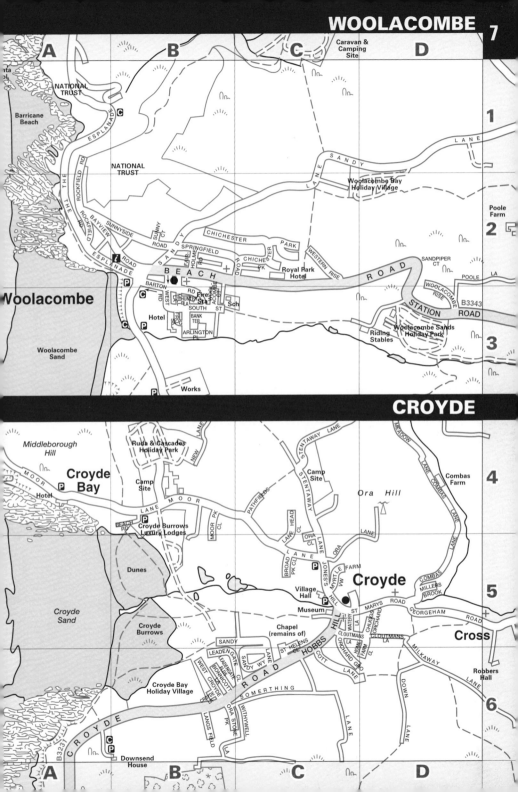

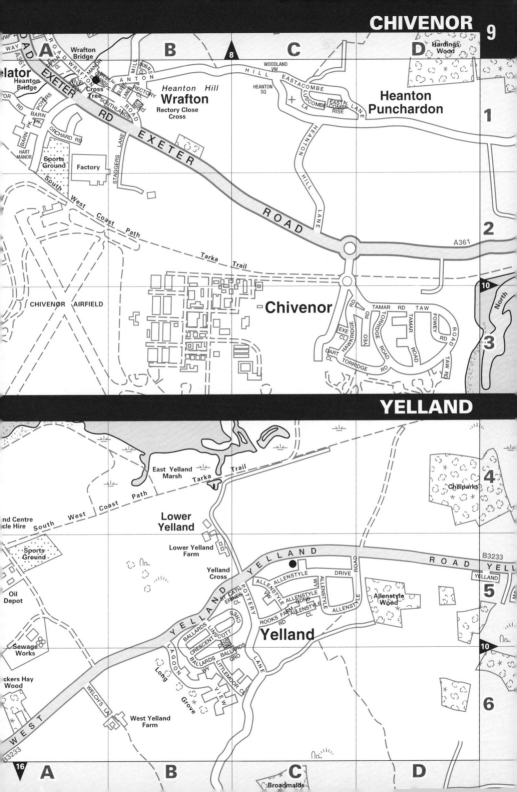

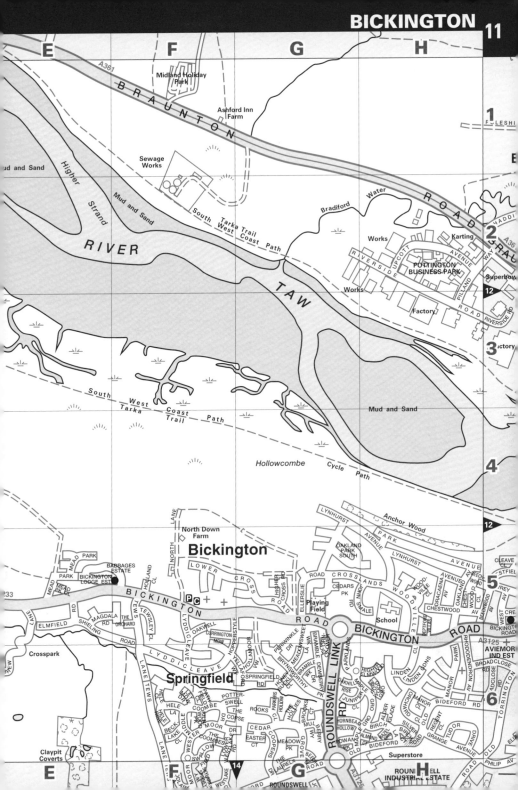

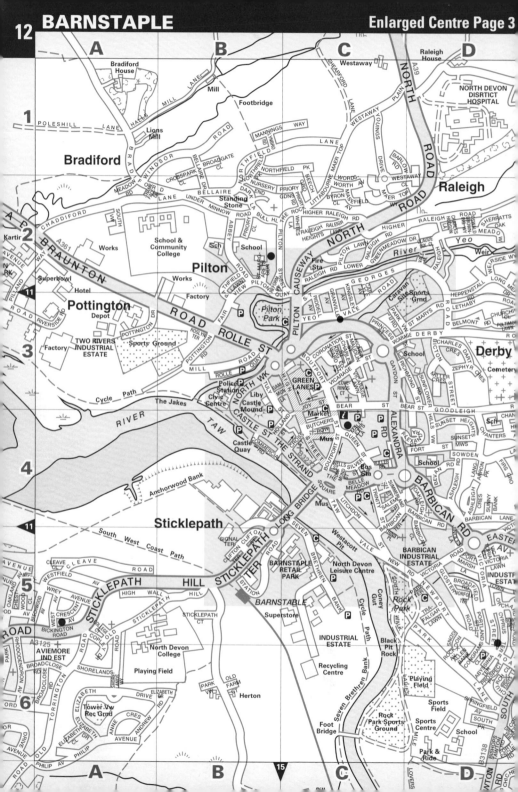

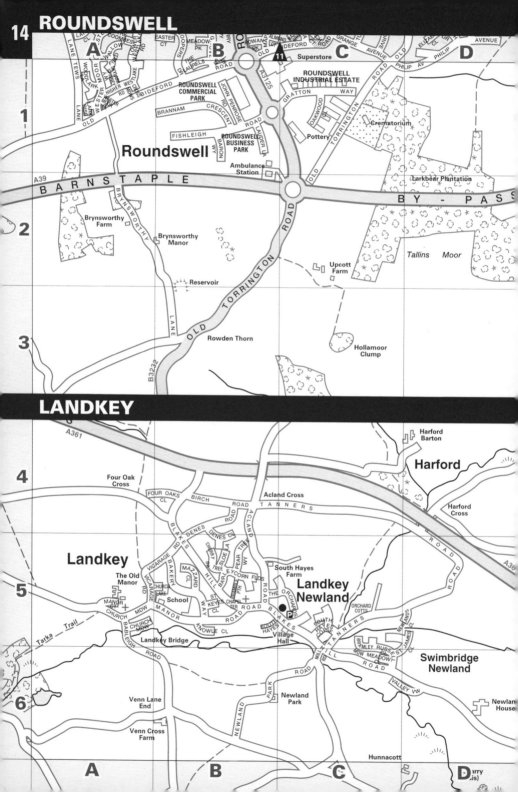

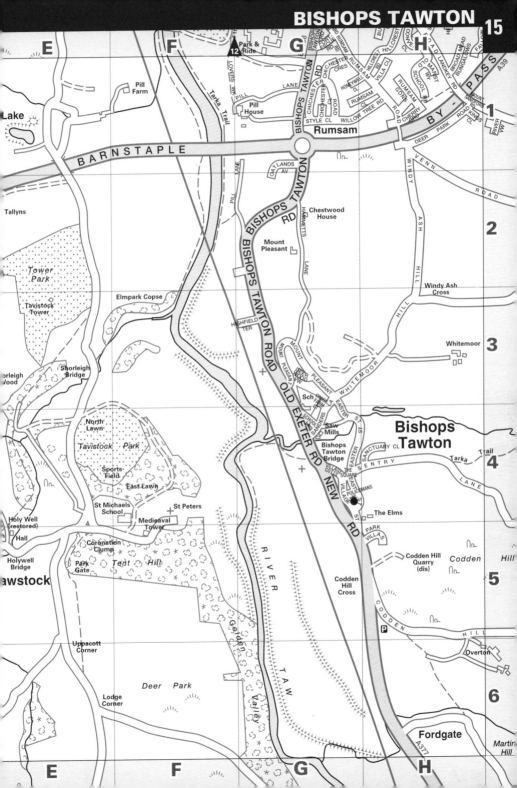

Appledore

Diddywell

Bloody Corner

Northam

Swimming Pool

Appledore Bridge

Richmond Farm

Whitehorse

Playing Field

Northcott Gdns

Oxmans

Northam Burrows Country Park

The Pill

Pimpley Bridge

Sandymere Sports Centre

School

Royal North Devon Golf Club

Underborough

The Fairways

Surf Bay Caravan Park

Eastbourne Ter

Aysha Gdns

Venton Dr

Karting

Cricket Grnd

Pebbleridge

Westbourne Ter

Youngaton Rd

Westward Ho!

Surfing

Pebble Ridge

Atlantic

Stanwell Hill

Buckleigh

Fairlea Residential Home

Daddon Hill Farm

Gresham Court

Buckleigh Laundry

Buckleigh Place Club

Carleton House

Cornborough

National Trust

Pusehill Rd

Heywood Rd

A386

B3236

Buckleigh Rd

Northam Burrows

Lundy Vw

Nelson Rd

Ennisfarne Rd

Merley Rd

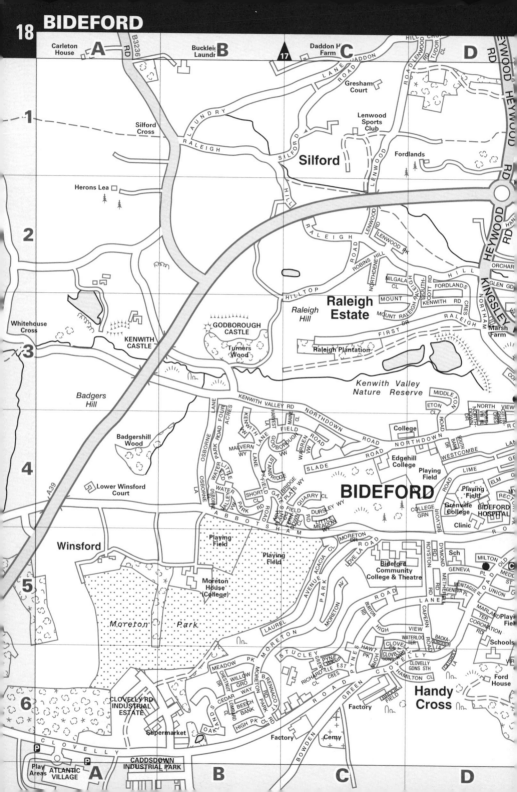

BIDEFORD

Carleton House — A

Buckleig Laundr — B

Daddon H Farm — C

D

B3236 RD

17

Silford Cross

Gresham Court

Lenwood Sports Club

HEYWOOD RD

HEYWOOD

Silford

Fordlands

LAUNDRY

RALEIGH

Herons Lea

SILFORD

LENWOOD

RALEIGH

LENWOOD RD

LENWOOD PK

ROAD

ROBINS HILL

NORTHDENE HILL

NILGALA CL

MOUNT RALEIGH

SOUTH RD

FORDLANDS

KENWITH RD

HILL

CRES

KINGSLEY

ORCHAR

GLEN RD

NORTHAM

Whitehouse Cross

KENWITH CASTLE

HILLTOP

GODBOROUGH CASTLE

Raleigh Hill

Raleigh Estate

MOUNT

FIRST

RALEIGH

Marsh Farm

Turners Wood

Raleigh Plantation

Badgers Hill

KENWITH VALLEY RD

Kenwith Valley Nature Reserve

MIDDLETON RD

ETON CL

NORTH VIEW

Badgershill Wood

OSBORNE

ROAD FOUR ACRES

LANE

LITTLE

HARVEST FIELD

MAIN

NORTHDOWN

College

NORTHDOWN

SOUTH BANK

WESTCOMBE

LIME

ELM

A39

Lower Winsford Court

OSBORNE LA

WATER PARK ROAD

KENWITH LANE

MALVERN WY

STANBY RIDGE

GODBOROUGH WY

WARREN WY

SLADE

ROAD

Edgehill College

Playing Field

Playing Field

Grenville College

RECT

BIDEFORD

BIDEFORD HOSPITAL

WATER VALLEY PARK

SHORT CL

G.A.T FIELD

BRIDGE FLATS WY

DURSLEY WY

QUARRY CL

LITTLE MEADOW WY

COLLEGE GRN

BELVOIR

Clinic

Winsford

ABBOTSHAM

ROAD

Playing Field

Playing Field

Moreton House (College)

MORETON DR

MORETON ROAD

AVENUE

ACACIA CL

LOVE LA

Bideford Community College & Theatre

ROYSTON

DYMOND RD

METHUEN

GENEVA

Sch

MILTON

PL

MEDI

ST

UNION

Moreton *Park*

LAUREL

PARK AV

MORETON

BURTON RD

HIGH

VIEW TER

LANE

CAPERN ROAD

MONTAGUE PL

CORONATION RD

MARLAND TER

Schools

Playi Fiel

Clovelly

MEADOW PK

CHESTNUT

WILLOW GRO

WAY

STUCLEY

GREENCLOSE

PYNE

RICHARDVILLE EST

CRES

HAWT

CLOVELLY

CLOVE

PK

CLOVELLY GDNS STH

HAMILTON CL

BACKA BOROUGH

Ford House

Handy Cross

Clovelly RD INDUSTRIAL ESTATE

CEDAR

PLUMB

BEECH BANK

HIGH PK

BRENNACO PARK RD

Factory

GREEN

ROAD

BOWDEN

PYNE

Factory

Cemy

Play Areas

ATLANTIC VILLAGE — A

CLOVELLY

CADDSDOWN INDUSTRIAL PARK

B

C

D

E   F   G   H

17

Westliving Farm

B3233

1

A39

The Cleve

PARK

LANE

LOWER

CLEEVE

CHICORAVE LA

Tarka Trail

Torridge Bridge

MAIN RD

Torridge Bridge

Ball Hill

TORRIDGE BRIDGE

ROAD

2

Orchard Hill

RIVERSIDE CL

RIVERSIDE

HILL

ROAD

ORCHARD RISE

Southcott

Colley Moor Plantation

ADRIAN CL

GLENFIELD

HARD

Sch

CHANTRY

GLENTORR RD

Council Offices

Cattle Market

King George V Playing Field

Rugby Grnd

MOUNT PLEASANT

CHANTERS

GOODWOOD PK DR

NEW

KINGSLEY

NEW

NO NEW

RD

3

Superstore

TORRIDGE

Sports Grnd

Victoria Park

CHARLES

STRAND

STRAND

ROAD

Burton Art Gallery

P Sch

Pottery

ROPEWALK

BRIDGELAND ST

BARNSTAPLE

Cemy

BARNSTAPLE

ROAD

4

COLD HARBOUR

LOWER

COOPER

GUNSTONE

QUEEN

HIGH

STREET

ETHERYNNE BROWN CL

OLD

GRAYNFYLDE DR

WEST VIEW AV

OLD

BARNSTAPLE

ROAD

ROAD

MINES

MAIN

Pannier Mkt

HYDE

SILVER ST

SILVER ST

BRIDGE ST

Town Hall Liby

BIDEFORD

Railway Sta Mus

SPRINGFIELD

GRANGE ROAD

Chudleigh Fort (remains of)

Park

CHUDLEIGH AV

EAST RIDGE

ATHES

NORTH HEATHFIELD

MERRI-FIELD

SOUTHFIELD RD

ROAD

BROADLANDS

SOUTH

CLEVE

KAREN

Sch

ROAD

5

THE

QUAY

RIVER

ROAD

BULL HL

TORRIDGE

Railway

TORRINGTON

TORRIDGE

GRANGE ROAD

SUNNYSIDE

CLIFTON

TORRINGTON

STREET

BROOK-FIELD

AVON

MINES

Sch

LANE

SENTRY CORNER

GAMMA

ALVERDISCOTT

ROAD

ROAD

SCHOOL

ABBOTS DR

BRECON

CLIVEDEN

OCHIL

TRENT

Sch

ROAD

6

DEVONSHIRE

PARK

Old Ford House

Depot

Wooder Wharf

Ford Rock

NEW

UPCOTT HL

A386

ROAD

Tarka Trail

KYNOCK INDUSTRIAL ESTATE

Depot

Pollyfield Centre

East-the-Water

Pollyfield Playing Field

Works

BARTON TORS

Factory

GOAMAN RD

CHURCHILL

ROAD

CHUBB

HILLCREST

CLIVEDEN

MONKS CL

TENNACOTT

ALVERDISCOTT ROAD INDUSTRIAL ESTATE

ROAD

GAMMATON ROAD

TENNACOTT LA

Works

E   F   G   H

Great Torrington

Crowbear

Taddiport

Pollard Hill

e Index includes some
nes for which there is
ufficient space on the
ps. These names are
icated by an * and are
owed by the nearest
oining thoroughfare.

bey Rd EX31   3 A1
oots Dr EX39   19 H6
ootsham Rd EX39   18 B4
ootts Hill EX33   8 D2
yssinia Ter EX32   12 D6
acia Cl EX39   18 C5
and Rd EX32   14 B4
elaide Ter EX34   4 C2
miral Ct EX39   17 E3
ian Cl EX39   19 E2
an Av EX32   13 F6
ert La EX32   3 C4
er Glade EX31   11 H6
xandra Cl EX32   3 D4
xandra Rd EX32   3 D3
xandra Ter EX34   4 C2
en Bank EX32   12 D6
enstyle EX31   9 C5
enstyle Dr EX31   9 C5
enstyle Gdns EX31   9 C5
enstyle Rd EX31   9 C5
enstyle Vw EX31   9 C5
enstyle Way EX31   9 C5
nalland St EX39   19 E5
nond Ct EX31   11 H6
na Pl EX39   16 B2
erdiscott Rd EX39   19 G5
erdiscott Rd Ind Est
X39   19 H6
ayas Way EX31   17 F4
drew Rd EX31   12 A6
drews Rd EX31   10 A5
ne Cres EX31   12 A6
stey Way EX39   16 C4
ole Orch EX38   20 B4
oledore Rd EX39   17 E2
oletree Cl EX32   13 F5
sley Ter EX34   4 C2
sley Villas EX34   4 D2
nor Cl EX34   4 C4
ade Rd EX32   7 B3
ngton Pl EX34   8 D3
ngton Ter EX33   17 A4
nada Way EX39   8 E2
a Rd EX33   8 E2
aleigh Cres EX32   12 D4
aleigh Rd EX32   3 D5
aley Ter EX34   4 C3
amead Gro EX33   8 C2
aplants Cl EX39   18 B4
ton Cres EX33   17 A4
antic Way EX34   17 A4
enue Rd EX34   4 C2
emore Ind Est
X31   12 A6
en La EX31   17 B3
en Rd EX39   19 F5
es Cl EX39   19 F5
sha Gdns EX39   17 C3
es La EX32   3 C4
bages Est EX31   11 E5
oleigh Rd EX32   14 A5
ckeborough La
X39   18 D5
kfield EX39   16 B3
ery Way EX32   14 B5
lards Cres EX31   9 B5
lards Gro EX31   9 B6
lards Way EX31   9 B6
moral Ter*,
Bannocks Park Rd
EX34   4 C3
k Ter EX34   7 B3
bican Cl EX31   3 D5
bican Ind Est
X32   3 D5
bican La EX32   12 D4
bican Rd EX32   3 D4
bican Ter EX32   3 C5
ley Gro EX38   20 D3
eycorn Flds EX32   14 B5
ow Rd EX31   12 C1
n Cl EX32   13 E6
n Pk EX33   9 A1
nfield Cl EX33   8 E3
nstable Rd EX34   5 F7

Barnstaple By-Pass
EX31,32   14 A2
Barnstaple Retail Pk
EX31   3 B6
Barnstaple St EX39   19 F5
Baron Way EX31   14 B1
Barton Av EX33   8 D4
Barton Gate La EX34   6 C2
Barton La EX33   8 D4
Barton Lane Cl EX33   8 D4
Barton Rd,
Barnstaple EX32   13 F5
Barton Rd,
Woolacombe EX34   7 B2
Barton Tors EX39   19 G6
Barum Arc EX32   3 C3
Barum Ct EX32   3 C5
Bassett Cl EX33   8 D3
Bassetts Cl EX39   17 E2
Bastards La EX38   20 C2
Bath Cl EX39   17 A3
Bath Hotel Rd EX39   17 A3
Bath Pl EX34   4 B2
Bay View Ct EX39   17 E4
Bay View Rd EX39   17 B4
Bayview Rd EX34   7 A2
Beach Rd,
Bideford EX39   17 C3
Beach Rd,
Braunton EX33   7 B4
Beach Rd,
Ilfracombe EX34   4 F2
Beach Rd,
Woolacombe EX34   7 B2
Beacon Heights EX33   8 D2
Bear St EX32   3 C3
Beards Rd EX31   10 B6
Becklake Cl EX31   11 F6
Bedford Row EX32   3 C4
Bedford St EX32   3 C4
Beech Bank EX39   18 B6
Beech Cl EX31   11 G6
Beech Gro,
Barnstaple EX31   12 C1
Beech Gro,
Braunton EX33   8 B2
Beech Pk EX31   10 B6
Beechfield Rd EX31   10 A6
Beechwood Av EX31   11 H5
Beechwood Cl EX31   11 H5
Bellaire EX31   12 B2
Bellaire Rd EX31   12 B1
Belle Meadow Ct EX32   3 C4
Belle Meadow Rd EX32   3 C4
Belles Cl EX31   10 B6
Belmont EX32   3 C2
Belmont Av,
Combe Martin EX34   6 C2
Belmont Av,
Ilfracombe EX34   4 B3
Belmont Rd,
Barnstaple EX32   3 D2
Belmont Rd,
Ilfracombe EX34   4 B3
Belvedere Rd EX34   4 C2
Belvoir Rd EX39   18 D4
Benson Dr EX39   17 F4
Berkeley Pl EX34   4 C2
Berry La EX34   6 B2
Berry Rd,
Barnstaple EX32   13 E5
Berry Rd,
Braunton EX33   8 E2
Bests La EX38   20 D2
Bevan Rd EX32   3 D4
Bias La EX33   8 D2
Bicclescombe Gdns
EX34   4 C4
Bicclescombe Park Rd
EX34   4 C4
Bickington Lodge Est
EX31   11 E5
Bickington Rd EX31   11 F5
Bicton St EX32   3 D4
Bideford Bri EX39   19 E5
Bidna La EX39   16 A4
Bingham Cres EX32   13 E4
Birch La EX31   11 H6
Birch Rd EX32   14 B4
Bishops Tawton Rd
EX32   15 G1
Blakeland Rd EX31   10 A6
Blakes Hill Rd EX32   14 B4
Blyth Ct EX39   17 A4
Bonnicott La EX34   7 B6
Boode Rd EX33   8 E2
Borough Rd,
Combe Martin EX34   6 C2

Borough Rd,
Great Torrington EX38   20 E2
Borough Vw EX38   20 E2
Boutport St EX31   3 B2
Bowden Grn EX39   18 C6
Bowering Ct EX32   12 D5
Bowling Green La
EX34   6 D3
Bradwell Rd EX34   4 B2
Brahms Way EX32   13 E4
Brake Wood Cl EX31   10 A6
Bramble Pth EX32   14 B5
Bramble Walk EX31   11 G6
Bramley Mdw EX32   14 C5
Brannam Cres EX31   14 B1
Brannams Sq EX32   3 C5
Brannams Walk EX32   3 C5
Braunton Rd EX31   11 F1
Brecon Cl EX39   19 G6
Brennacott Rd EX39   18 B6
Brewer Rd EX32   13 E5
Bridge La EX39   16 D3
Bridge Plats Way EX39   18 C4
Bridge St EX39   19 E5
Bridgeland St EX39   19 E4
Britannia Way EX39   17 D3
Britten Dr EX32   13 E4
Brittons Cl EX33   8 D3
Broad Cl EX33   8 C3
Broad La EX39   16 A3
Broad Mead Bungalows
EX32   15 H1
Broad Park Av EX34   4 A3
Broad Park Cl EX33   7 C5
Broad Park Cres EX34   4 B3
Broad St EX34   4 D2
Broadclose Rd EX31   12 A6
Broadfield Rd EX32   12 D5
Broadgate Cl,
Barnstaple EX31   12 B1
Broadgate Cl,
Braunton EX33   8 D2
Broadlands,
Bideford EX39   19 G5
Broadlands,
Northam EX39   17 E2
Broadway EX31   10 C6
Broady Strap EX31   10 C5
Brookdale Av EX34   4 B2
Brookfield Cl EX31   18 C6
Brookfield Cl EX33   8 D3
Brookfield Pl EX31   4 B2
Brookfield EX39   19 F5
Brooks Cl EX31   11 G6
Brynsworthy La EX31   14 A2
Brynsworthy Pk EX31   11 G6
Buckleigh Rd EX39   17 B4
Bude St EX31   16 B2
Bull Ct EX31   3 B3
Bull Hill,
Barnstaple EX31   12 B2
Bull Hill,
Bideford EX39   19 E5
Buller Rd EX32   3 C4
Burlington Cl EX32   13 E6
Burlington Gro EX32   13 E6
Burnside EX34   4 B4
Burrough Rd EX39   17 E4
Burrow Rd EX34   4 B3
Burrows Cl EX33   8 C3
Burrows Pk EX33   8 C3
Burton Rd EX39   18 C5
Burwood La EX38   20 F2
Burwood Rd EX38   20 E2
Business Pk EX34   4 F2
Butchers Row EX31   3 B3
Buttercombe La EX32   8 F1
Buttgarden St EX39   19 E5
Butts Path EX33   8 D2
Buzzacott Cl EX34   6 F4
Buzzacott La EX34   6 F4
Byeways Cl EX31   10 C6
Byron Cl EX31   12 C2

Caddsdown Ind Pk
EX39   18 A6
Caddywell La EX38   20 E3
Caddywell Mdw EX38   20 E3
Caen Fld EX33   8 C3
Caen Gdns EX33   8 C2
Caen St EX33   8 D2
Cairn Rd EX34   4 B4
Cairn Side EX34   4 C4
Calf St EX38   20 D2
Calvesford Cl EX38   20 E2
Calvesford Rd EX38   20 E2
Cambridge Gro EX34   4 D2
Campion Dr EX32   13 G4

Capern Cl EX33   8 E4
Capern Rd EX39   18 D5
Capstone Par EX34   4 C1
Capstone Pl*,
Capstone Rd EX34   4 D1
Capstone Rd EX34   4 D1
Carlyle Av EX32   3 C1
Carrington Ter EX32   3 C1
Castle Hill EX34   4 D2
Castle Hill Av EX34   4 D2
Castle Hill Gdns EX38   20 D3
Castle La EX38   20 D3
Castle Park Rd EX32   13 G5
Castle Pk Ind Est
EX32   13 G6
Castle Quay Ct EX31   3 A4
Castle St,
Torrington EX38   20 D3
Castle St,
Bideford EX39   17 E4
Castle St,
Combe Martin EX34   6 E3
Castle Ter EX34   4 D2
Cat La EX34   4 F3
Cater Rd EX32   12 D5
Catshole La EX34   4 F3
Causeway Cl EX39   17 E3
Cavie Cres EX33   8 B2
Cavie Rd EX33   8 B2
Caynton Ct EX38   20 C3
Cedar Gro EX31   11 G6
Cedar Way EX39   18 B6
Cedars Pk EX31   11 G5
Century Dr EX39   17 D4
Ceramic Ter EX32   3 C5
Chaddiford La EX31   12 A2
Chaloners Rd EX33   8 D1
Chambercombe La
EX34   4 F3
Chambercombe Park Rd
EX34   4 E2
Chambercombe Rd
EX34   4 E2
Chambercombe Ter
EX34   4 E2
Champernowne Cres
EX34   4 E3
Chandlers Ct EX39   16 D3
Chandlers Way EX34   4 C4
Channel Vw EX34   4 E3
Chanters Hill EX32   12 D4
Chanters Rd EX39   19 E3
Chantry Av EX39   19 E3
Chapel La EX33   6 D3
Chapel St EX33   8 C2
Chapel Ter EX32   14 B5
Charles Av EX39   19 E4
Charles Dart Cres EX32   3 D2
Charles Hudson La
EX32   12 D2
Charles St EX39   3 C2
Cherry Arbor EX32   15 H1
Cherry Gro EX32   15 H1
Cherry Pk EX39   17 F1
Cherry Tree Dr EX32   14 B5
Chestnut Cl EX33   8 D2
Chestnut Cl EX38   18 B6
Chestwood Av EX31   11 H5
Chestwood Cl EX31   11 H5
Chichester Cl,
Barnstaple EX32   15 G1
Chichester Cl,
Bideford EX39   16 D2
Chichester Cl,
Ilfracombe EX34   4 B4
Chichester Cres EX32   15 G1
Chichester Pk EX34   7 B2
Chichester Rd EX34   7 B2
Chichester Way EX39   17 A4
Chichesters Yd EX33   8 D2
Chilpark EX31   10 A5
Chingswell St EX39   19 E4
Chircombe La EX39   19 E1
Chivenor EX31   9 D4
Chope Rd EX39   17 E4
Chopes Cl EX39   19 G6
Chubb Rd EX31   19 G6
Chudleigh Av EX39   19 F5
Chudleigh Rd EX39   19 F5
Chuggs Orch EX32   3 B2
Church Cl EX39   12 D6
Church Hill,
Barnstaple EX31   10 B5
Church Hill,
Ilfracombe EX34   4 B3
Church La EX38   20 C3

Church Lake EX32   14 B5
Church Mdw EX32   14 A5
Church Rd EX34   4 B2
Church St,
Braunton EX33   8 D1
Church St,
Combe Martin EX34   6 D3
Church St,
Ilfracombe EX34   4 B2
Church Walk EX39   19 E5
Churchfield EX39   16 B2
Churchill Cl EX32   12 D3
Churchill Rd EX39   19 F6
Churchill Way EX39   17 E4
Claude Dix Cl EX32   12 D2
Cleave Cl EX31   12 A5
Cleave Pk EX31   10 C5
Cleave Rd EX31   12 A5
Cleavewood Dr EX39   19 G5
Clevelands Pk EX39   17 E4
Clifton St,
Barnstaple EX31   3 A5
Clifton St,
Bideford EX39   19 F5
Clifton Ter EX31   3 A6
Clinton Rd EX32   13 E6
Cliveden Rd EX39   19 G6
Cloutmans La EX33   7 C5
Clovelly Cl EX39   18 C5
Clovelly Gdns North
EX39   18 C6
Clovelly Gdns South
EX39   18 A6
Clovelly Rd EX39   18 A6
Clovelly Rd Ind Est
EX39   18 A6
Clover Way EX32   13 G4
Cluden Rd EX39   17 D4
Codden Hill EX32   15 H5
Cold Harbour EX32   19 E4
College Dr EX39   17 B4
College Ct EX31   12 A5
College Grn EX39   18 D4
Colley Park Rd EX33   8 D3
Combas La EX33   7 D4
Combe Pk EX34   4 D3
Combrew La EX31   10 D5
Comers La EX34   6 E3
Commercial Rd EX31   3 A4
Commodore Cl EX39   17 D3
Comyn Hill EX39   4 D3
Concord Dr EX32   13 E3
Coney Av EX32   13 E5
Coney Park La EX34   6 E3
Congrams Cl EX32   12 D6
Connaught Pl EX32   3 C4
Constitution Hill EX32   13 E4
Convent Cl EX32   13 E6
Cooper St EX39   19 E4
Coopers Dr EX31   11 G6
Copley Dr EX31   12 A5
Coppice Cl,
Barnstaple EX32   13 G5
Coppice Cl,
Fremington EX31   10 C5
Coppice Gate EX32   13 F6
Copps St EX39   18 D3
Coral Av EX39   17 C3
Corilhead Rd EX33   8 D1
Cornborough Rd EX39   17 A4
Corner La EX34   6 E3
Cornflower Cl EX31   11 G6
Cornmkt St EX38   20 D3
Coronation Rd EX39   18 D5
Coronation St EX32   3 B2
Coronation Ter EX34   4 D2
Corporation Cres EX32   12 D6
Corporation St EX32   13 E6
Corporation Ter EX32   12 D6
Cott La EX33   7 C6
Cottingham Cres EX39   18 D3
Cow La EX34   4 C2
Cow Park Ter EX39   17 E3
Crescent Av EX31   12 A5
Crofts Lea Pk EX34   4 E3
Croftswood Gdns EX34   4 E3
Croftswood Villas EX34   4 E3
Cromwell Cl EX38   20 F2
Cross Cl EX31   10 A6
Cross Farm Ct EX32   15 G3
Cross Mdws EX31   14 A1
Cross Pk EX34   4 B2
Cross St,
Barnstaple EX31   3 B4
Cross St,
Bideford EX39   17 E3
Cross St,
Combe Martin EX34   6 C1

Crosslands EX31 11 G5
Crosspark Cl EX31 12 B2
Crow Vw EX32 13 E3
Crowbeare Mdw EX38 20 E1
Croyde La EX33 7 B6
Croyde Rd EX33 7 A6
Currington Mdw EX31 11 F5
Curve Acre EX33 8 E3
Cyprus Ter EX32 12 D5

Daddon Hill EX39 18 C1
Daneshay EX39 17 F3
Dark La EX31 12 B2
Dart Cl EX31 9 C3
Dartington Cl EX38 20 E2
Dartington Flds EX38 20 E1
Davids Cl EX33 8 D3
Deans Cl EX39 17 E3
Deer Park Rd EX32 15 H1
Deer Wood Vw EX32 15 G3
Denes Cl EX32 14 B4
Denes Rd EX32 14 B5
Deptford Villas EX31 11 H5
Derby Rd EX32 3 D2
Devonshire Pk EX39 19 E6
Dewberry Dr EX31 11 G6
Diamond St EX32 3 C4
Dickshill La EX38 20 D3
Diddy Ct EX39 17 F3
Diddywell Cl EX39 17 F2
Diddywell Rd EX39 17 E3
Doe Ct EX38 20 D2
Doggie La EX34 5 A5
Dolphin Ct EX39 17 D3
Doone Way EX34 4 C4
Dovedale Cl EX34 4 F3
Down La,
  Braunton EX33 8 E2
Down La, Croyde EX33 7 D6
Downs Rd EX39 16 D2
Dracaena Av EX31 11 H5
Drake Cl EX39 17 A4
Drapers Cl EX34 6 E4
Dudley Way EX39 17 A4
Dune View Rd EX33 8 B2
Dune Vw EX39 17 B3
Dunns Cl EX33 8 E4
Durrant Cl EX39 19 E1
Durrant La EX39 19 E1
Dursley Way EX39 18 C4
Dyers Cl EX33 8 D2
Dymond Rd EX39 18 D5

East Hill EX33 8 D2
East Meadow Rd EX33 8 B1
East Park Rd EX32 13 F5
East Ridge Vw EX39 19 F5
East St,
  Barnstaple EX32 15 G4
East St, Braunton EX33 8 D3
East St,
  Torrington EX38 20 E2
Eastacombe La EX31 9 C1
Eastacombe Rise EX31 9 C1
Eastbourne Ter EX39 17 C3
Easter Ct EX31 11 G6
Easter St EX32 15 G4
Eastern Av EX32 12 D5
Ebberley Lawn EX32 3 D3
Eddys La EX32 12 D6
Edwards Dr EX39 17 C3
Elgar Cl EX32 13 E4
Elizabeth Cl EX31 12 A6
Elizabeth Dr EX31 12 A6
Ellerslie Rd EX31 11 G5
Elliot Cl EX32 13 F5
Elm Gro EX39 18 D4
Elmdale Rd EX39 19 E3
Elmfield Rd EX31 11 E5
Elmlea Av EX31 10 B5
Ennisfarne Rd EX39 17 A3
Ensign Ct EX39 17 D3
Eskil Pl EX38 20 C2
Estuary Vw EX39 9 A6
Estuary Way EX39 17 E2
Ethelwynne Brown Cl
  EX39 19 F4
Eton Cl EX39 18 D3
Exe Cl EX31 9 C3
Exeter Rd EX39 8 D3

Fair Vw EX31 3 A2
Fairacre Av EX32 13 E6
Fairfax Way EX38 20 F2
Fairfield EX34 4 D3
Fairholme Rd EX34 7 B2
Fairlea Cres EX39 17 D4
Fairlynch Cl EX33 8 A1
Fairlynch Gro EX33 8 B1
Fairlynch La EX33 8 A1
Fairway EX39 16 A3
Fallowfields EX32 13 F6
Fern Cl EX34 4 C3
Fern Pk EX34 4 C3
Fern Way EX34 4 C3

Ferndown Cl EX39 18 C4
Field Cl EX33 8 C3
Field La EX33 8 C3
Firs Gro EX32 12 D4
First Raleigh EX39 18 C3
Fishleigh Rd EX31 14 B1
Five Turnings EX34 6 D2
Flexa Pk EX34 6 D2
Forches Av EX32 13 E4
Ford Rise EX39 18 E6
Fordlands Cres EX39 18 D2
Fore St, Bideford EX39 17 E4
Fore St,
  Ilfracombe EX34 4 C2
Fore St,
  Torrington EX38 20 D2
Foreland Ho*,
  Foreland Vw EX34 4 B4
Foreland Vw EX34 4 B3
Fort Hill EX32 13 E4
Fort Mead Cl EX32 3 D3
Fort St EX32 3 D4
Fort Ter EX32 3 D4
Fortescue Cl EX33 8 D3
Fortescue Rd EX32 12 D6
Fortescue Rd EX34 4 C2
Fosketh Hill EX39 17 B4
Four Acres EX39 18 B4
Four Oaks Cl EX34 14 A4
Fowey Rd EX31 9 D3
Foxbeare Rd EX34 4 F2
Foxglove Cl EX32 13 G4
Foxhill EX33 8 C3
Foxhole La EX34 17 A4
Francis Dr EX39 17 A4
Franklyn Av EX32 8 D3
Frankmarsh Pk EX32 13 E3
Frankmarsh Rd EX32 12 D3
Fremington Quay
  EX31 10 C4
Frog La EX33 8 D1
Frog St EX34 7 B3
Furze Hill Rd EX34 4 C3

Galleon Way EX39 17 D3
Galloway La EX33 8 C4
Gammaton Rd EX39 19 G5
Gammon La EX31 3 B3
Garden Cl EX33 8 B2
Gas La EX38 20 D2
Gate Field Rd EX39 18 B4
Gaydon St EX32 3 C2
Genesis La EX34 6 D2
Geneva Cl EX39 18 D5
Geneva Pl EX39 18 D5
George St EX32 3 B2
Georgeham Rd EX33 7 D5
Gibbs La EX39 16 B2
Gilbert Gro EX34 4 D2
Gipsy La EX34 4 E2
Glazon Way EX39 17 E2
Glebe Flds EX39 17 E4
Glebelands EX33 9 B1
Glen Gdns EX39 18 D2
Glenburnie Rd EX39 19 E3
Glenfield Rd EX39 19 E2
Glengarth Cl EX39 19 E1
Glentorr Rd EX39 19 E2
Gloster Rd EX32 3 D6
Goaman Rd EX39 19 G6
Godborough Vw EX39 18 B4
Goats Hill Rd EX39 17 E4
Golf Links Rd EX39 17 B3
Goodgates Cl EX33 8 B2
Goodgates Cres EX33 8 B2
Goodgates Gro EX33 8 B2
Goodgates Pk EX33 8 B2
Goodgates Rd EX33 8 B2
Goodleigh Rd EX32 12 D3
Goodwood Park Rd
  EX39 19 E1
Gorwell Rd EX33 13 E3
Gould Cl EX32 13 E5
Gould Rd EX32 13 E5
Grange Av EX31 11 H6
Grange Rd EX39 19 F5
Granville Av EX33 3 B1
Granville Rd EX34 4 D2
Gratton Way EX31 14 C1
Graynfylde Dr EX39 19 F4
Great Burrow Rise
  EX39 17 E3
Great Field Gdns EX33 8 C3
Green Gdns EX39 17 D4
Green La,
  Barnstaple EX32 3 B2
Green La,
  Bideford EX39 16 B2
Green La,
  Braunton EX33 8 E2
Green Lanes EX31 12 C3
Green Lanes
  Shopping Centre
  EX31 3 B3
Greenacre EX33 8 B2

Greenacre Cl EX39 17 F3
Greenbank EX38 20 F2
Greenbank EX33 20 F1
Greenbank Rd EX32 13 E5
Greenclose Rd EX34 4 B2
Greenmeadow Dr
  EX32 3 C1
Greenways EX34 4 B3
Greig Dr EX32 13 E4
Grenville Est Cres
  EX39 18 C6
Grenville St EX39 19 E4
Grenville Ter EX39 17 F3
Greysand Cres EX34 16 A1
Gribble Cl EX32 13 E5
Griggs Cl EX39 17 F4
Griggs Gdn EX31 10 B6
Grosvenor St EX32 3 D3
Gubbins La EX33 8 D3

Halls Mill La EX31 12 A1
Halsdon Ter EX38 20 C3
Hamilton Cl EX39 18 C6
Hammetts La EX32 15 G2
Hangman Path EX32 6 B1
Hanson Pk EX39 18 D2
Hardaway Head EX32 3 C4
Hart Manor EX33 9 A1
Harvest La EX39 18 B3
Hatchmoor Common La
  EX38 20 F1
Hatchmoor Est EX38 20 E2
Hatchmoor La Ind Est
  EX38 20 F1
Hatchmoor Rd EX38 20 E2
Hawkridge Rd EX31 9 C3
Hawley Cl EX32 13 E4
Hawley Manor EX32 13 E4
Hawthorn Av EX34 4 E3
Hawthorn Pk EX39 18 C6
Hawthorn Rd EX32 13 G5
Haydn Cl EX32 13 E4
Hayne Pk EX32 13 E4
Hazel Av EX33 8 E2
Hazel Gro EX31 11 H6
Heal Park Cres EX31 10 A6
Heanton Hill EX33 9 B1
Heanton Hill La EX31 9 C1
Heanton Sq EX31 9 C1
Heanton St EX33 8 D3
Heathfield Rd EX39 19 G5
Hele Cl EX31 11 F6
Hele La EX31 11 F6
Hele Rise EX31 11 F6
Heppenstall Rd EX32 3 D1
Hermitage Rd EX34 4 B2
Heron Ct EX32 13 H4
Heywood Av EX32 13 E6
Heywood Rd EX39 17 E4
Hierns La EX34 4 D2
High Park Cl EX39 18 B6
High St,
  Barnstaple EX31 3 B2
High St, Bideford EX39 19 E4
High St,
  Combe Martin EX34 6 D3
High St,
  Ilfracombe EX34 4 C2
High St,
  Torrington EX38 20 D3
High Vw EX39 18 C5
High Wall EX31 12 A5
Highbury Hill EX39 17 F2
Highbury Rd EX32 13 F6
Higher Church St EX32 3 C5
Higher Cross Rd EX31 11 G5
Higher Elmwood EX31 11 H6
Higher Gunstone EX39 19 E4
Higher Hillside Rd EX34 4 F2
Higher Maudlin St
  EX32 3 C2
Higher Park Rd EX32 8 E2
Higher Raleigh Rd
  EX31 17 D2
Higher Rd EX31 10 B5
Higher Slade Rd EX34 5 A5
Higher Westlake Rd
  EX31 14 A1
Highfield EX39 17 D4
Highfield Cl EX32 12 D4
Highfield Gdns EX34 6 D2
Highfield Rd EX34 4 C2
Highfield Ter EX31 15 F3
Highfield Ter*,
  Highfield Rd EX34 4 D2
Hillcliff Ter EX39 16 A1
Hillcrest Rd,
  Barnstaple EX32 13 E6
Hillcrest Rd,
  Bideford EX39 19 G6
Hillington EX34 4 B3
Hills Vw,
  Barnstaple EX32 3 D3
Hills Vw,
  Braunton EX33 8 D2

Hillsborough Park Rd
  EX34 4 F2
Hillsborough Rd EX34 4 D2
Hillsborough Ter EX34 4 D2
Hillside Rd EX34 4 F2
Hilltop Rd EX39 18 C3
Hobbs Hill EX33 7 C6
Hodges Walk EX38 20 E2
Holdstone Way EX34 6 F4
Hollamoor Vw EX31 11 G6
Holland Cl EX31 11 F5
Holland Park Av EX32 6 E2
Holland St EX31 3 B4
Holland Walk EX31 3 B3
Hollowtree Ct EX32 13 E6
Hollowtree Rd EX32 13 E5
Holwill Dr EX38 20 D3
Home Farm Cl EX33 7 C6
Home Farm Rd EX31 10 A6
Homer Cres EX33 8 B1
Homer Rd EX33 8 B1
Homer Rd EX33 8 A1
Honestone St EX39 19 E5
Honey St EX39 17 E3
Honeysuckle Cl EX31 11 G6
Honeywell Cl EX32 15 G1
Hoopers Way EX38 20 F2
Hopperstyle EX31 11 F6
Hopton Dr EX38 20 F2
Hornbeam Hollow
  EX31 11 G6
Horne Park Av EX34 4 C3
Horne Park Rd EX34 4 C3
Horne Rd EX34 4 B2
Hornebrook Av*,
  Horne Rd EX34 4 B3
Hostle Park Rd EX34 4 C2
Hostle Pk EX34 4 C2
Howard Av EX32 13 E5
Howard Av Ind Est
  EX32 13 E5
Hows Cotts*,
  Nutteberry Hill EX39 19 F5
Hubbastone Rd EX39 16 B4
Hughes Av EX32 13 E6
Hunter La EX34 7 B3
Hunters Wood EX38 20 F3
Hyfield Pl EX39 19 E5

Irsha St EX39 16 A1
Irving Cl EX33 8 B2

J H Taylor Dr EX39 17 F3
Jackets La EX39 17 E3
Jewell Cres EX32 13 E3
Jingles La EX32 12 D4
John Gay Cl EX32 13 E4
John Gay Rd EX32 13 E4
John Howe Cl EX38 20 D3
John Penrose Rd EX31 14 B1
John Smale Rd EX31 11 G5
Jones's Hill EX33 7 C5
Jordan Cl EX32 13 E6
Joy St EX31 3 B3
Jubilee Rd EX39 16 A1
Juniper Cl EX31 11 G6
Juries La EX38 20 D2

Kala Fair EX39 17 C3
Karen Cl EX39 19 G5
Kenwith Castle EX39 18 A3
Kenwith Valley Rd
  EX39 18 B3
Kenwith Vw EX39 18 B4
Kestrel Way EX32 13 H4
Kiln Close La EX39 16 D2
Kiln La,
  Barnstaple EX32 3 C5
Kiln La,
  Combe Martin EX34 6 E4
Kilnwood Pk EX31 11 F6
King Edward St EX32 3 C2
King St, Bideford EX39 19 E4
King St,
  Combe Martin EX34 6 C2
Kingfisher Dr EX32 13 H4
Kings Cl EX32 15 H1
Kings Rd EX32 3 B2
Kingsacre EX33 8 B2
Kingsley Av,
  Barnstaple EX32 3 C1
Kingsley Av,
  Ilfracombe EX34 4 C4
Kingsley Ct EX39 17 B4
Kingsley Pk EX39 17 C3
Kingsley Rd,
  Appledore EX39 16 A3
Kingsley Rd,
  Bideford EX39 18 D2
Kingsley Rd,
  Westward Ho EX39 17 B4
Kingsley St EX31 19 E4
Kingsmead Dr EX38 20 F2
Kingston Av EX34 6 C2

Kneller Cl EX34 4
Knightsfield Rise EX39 17
Knowle Cl EX34 14
Knowle Gdns EX34 6
Kynock Ind Est EX39 19

Laburnum Dr EX32 13
Ladder La EX34 6
Ladies Mile EX32 3
Lagoon Vw EX32 9
Lakenham Hill EX39 17
Lamb Pk EX34 4
Landkey Rd EX32 13
Lane End Cl EX32 16
Lane End Pk EX32 13
Lane End Rd EX39 16
Lane Field Rd EX39 18
Lane Head Cl EX33 7
Langarron Pk EX32 12
Langleigh La EX34 4
Langleigh Pk EX34 4
Langleigh Rd EX34 4
Langs Fld EX33 7
Lansdown Pk EX31 14
Lark Rise EX31 14
Larkspur Gdns EX32 13
Larkstone Cres EX34 4
Larkstone Gdns EX34 4
Larkstone La EX34 4
Larkstone Ter EX34 4
Lauder La EX31 14
Lauderdale Dr EX32 13
Laundry La EX39 18
Laurel Av EX39 18
Leadengate Cl EX33 7
Leadengate Flds EX33 7
Leigh Rd EX34 6
Lenards Rd EX39 18
Lenwood Pk EX39 18
Lenwood Rd EX39 18
Lethaby Rd EX32 12
Lever Cl EX39 17
Ley Meadow Dr EX31 11
Lily Cl EX39 17
Lilybridge EX39 17
Lime Gro EX39 18
Limers Hill EX38 20
Limers La EX39 18
Limetree Gro EX39 8
Linden Cl,
  Barnstaple EX31 11
Linden Cl,
  Braunton EX33 8
Linden Cl,
  Torrington EX38 20
Linden Gdns EX31 11
Linhay Dr EX31 10
Link Ho EX39 17
Linscott Cres EX31 9
Litchdon Cotts EX32 3
Litchdon La EX32 3
Litchdon St EX32 3
Littabourne Maer Top
  EX31 12
Little Field Cl EX32 13
Little Fld EX39 18
Little Meadow Way
  EX39 18
Littlemoor Cl EX31 9
Locks Cl EX33 8
Lombard St EX32 18
Long Bri EX31 3
Long La EX39 17
Long Meadow Dr
  EX32 12
Longfield EX39 18
Longfield Cl EX33 8
Longfield Ter EX34 4
Louise Ter EX38 20
Love La EX39 18
Loverings Ct EX32 3
Lovers La EX39 16
Lovers Walk EX31 15
Lower Burwood Rd
  EX38 20
Lower Church St EX32 3
Lower Cleave,
  Bideford EX39 19
Lower Cleave,
  Braunton EX33 8
Lower Cross Rd EX31 11
Lower Dean La EX31 9
Lower Gaydon St EX32 3
Lower Gunstone EX39 19
Lower Maudlin St
  EX32 3
Lower Meddon St
  EX39 19
Lower Moor EX32 13
Lower Park Rd EX32 13
Lower Raleigh Rd
  EX32 17
Lower Westlake Rd
  EX31 13
Lundy Cl EX32 12

22

dy Vw EX39 17 D4
combe La EX31 9 C1
icleave EX31 11 F5
urst Av EX31 11 G4
r Top Way EX31 12 C2
dala Rd EX31 11 E5
dalene Lawn EX32 3 C2
nolia Cl EX32 13 H5
den St EX31 3 B4
n Rd EX39 19 F4
ne Cl EX39 18 C4
etts La EX32 3 C4
ern Way EX39 18 B4
nings Way EX31 12 B1
or Cl,
 unton EX33 8 E4
or Cl,
 mington EX31 10 B5
or Cl,
 cklepath EX31 11 H6
or Ct EX32 14 A5
or Rd EX31 11 H6
or Rd EX32 14 B5
grove Ter EX32 3 C2
ne Par,
 pledore EX39 16 B3
ne Par,
 ow EX39 16 D3
iners Way EX39 16 A2
st Way EX31 15 H1
ket Pl EX31 19 E5
ket St,
 nstaple EX31 3 B3
ket St,
 eford EX39 16 B2
ket St,
 icombe EX34 4 C2
and Ter EX39 18 D5
borough Cl*,
 rlborough EX34 4 C3
borough Ct EX39 19 E3
borough Pk EX34 4 C2
borough Way
 34 4 D3
en Ct EX39 19 E6
sh La EX39 16 D3
in Rd EX32 13 E3
ines Rd EX32 20 F2
wood Ct EX38 20 D2
field Av EX31 12 C2
d Park Cl EX31 11 E5
d Pk EX31 11 E5
dow Cl,
 nstaple EX32 14 C6
dow Cl,
 icombe EX34 4 C4
dow La,
 eford EX39 16 D3
dow La,
 unton EX33 7 D4
dow La,
 nstaple EX31 11 G6
dow Pk,
 eford EX39 18 B6
dow Rd EX31 12 A2
dowsweet La
 31 11 G6
dowville Rd EX39 19 E3
ard Ho EX32 3 D4
don St EX39 18 D5
ting St EX39 18 D5
dian Pl EX34 4 C2
ey Rd EX39 17 A3
maid Cross EX31 3 B2
ifield Rd EX39 19 G5
ylees Dr EX32 13 E6
ythorn Rd EX31 10 A6
erell Rd EX39 18 D5
dle Coombe Dr
 31 11 F6
dleton Rd EX39 18 D3
away La EX33 7 D6
Head Ter EX34 4 C2
Hill EX31 10 D5
La, Braunton EX33 8 E4
La,
 olacombe EX34 7 B3
Mdw EX34 6 D3
Rd,
 nstaple EX31 12 B3
Rd,
 nington EX31 10 B6
Rd, Landkey EX32 14 C6
St, Bideford EX39 19 E4
St,
 rington EX38 20 B3
Stile EX33 8 E3
rds Hill EX39 16 D2
nnium Way EX37 17 C3
er Cres EX32 3 D2

Millers Brook EX33 7 D5
Milton Pl EX39 18 D5
Mines Rd EX39 19 G5
Mint Park Rd EX33 8 A1
Mondeville Way EX39 17 E3
Monks Cl EX39 19 H6
Montague Pl EX39 18 D5
Montpelier Mws*,
 Montpelier Rd EX34 4 C4
Montpelier Rd EX34 4 C2
Montpelier Ter EX34 4 D2
Moor La,
 Braunton EX33 8 A3
Moor La, Croyde EX33 7 B4
Moor Lea EX33 8 E3
Moor Park Cl EX33 7 B5
Moorland Ter EX38 20 B2
Moory Mdw EX34 6 C2
Moreton Av EX39 18 C5
Moreton Dr EX39 18 C5
Moreton Park Rd EX39 18 B6
Morwenna Park Rd
 EX39 17 E3
Mount Pleasant,
 Barnstaple EX32 15 G3
Mount Pleasant,
 Bideford EX39 19 F3
Mount Raleigh EX39 18 C3
Mount Raleigh Dr
 EX39 18 C3
Mount Sandford Rd
 EX32 15 H1
Mount Vw EX34 4 D2
Mowstead Rd EX33 8 A2
Mulberry Way EX31 11 G6
Mullacott Cross Ind Est
 EX34 5 C8
Mutton La EX34 20 C4
Myrtle Cott Rd EX39 17 F2
Myrtle Farm Vw EX33 7 C5
Myrtle Gdns EX39 19 E4
Myrtle Gro EX39 18 D4
Myrtle St EX39 16 B3
Nelson Dr EX39 17 B3
Nelson Rd EX39 17 A3
Netherton La EX34 6 E2
New Barnstable Rd
 EX34 4 D2
New Bldgs EX32 3 C2
New Ct EX39 19 E3
New La EX33 7 B4
New Quay St EX39 16 B3
New Rd,
 Barnstaple EX32 3 C6
New Rd,
 Bideford EX39 19 E6
New Rd,
 Bishops Tawton EX32 15 G4
New Rd, Instow EX39 16 D3
New Rd,
 Torrington EX38 20 D2
New Row EX39 19 E4
New St,
 Appledore EX39 16 B3
New St, Bideford EX39 19 E4
New St,
 Torrington EX38 20 B2
Newberry Cl EX34 6 A1
Newberry Hill EX34 6 A2
Newberry Rd EX34 6 B2
Newbridge Ct EX39 19 E2
Newland Park Rd
 EX32 14 B6
Newlands Cl EX32 14 C5
Newport Rd EX32 12 D5
Newport Ter EX39 19 F5
Newton Rd EX39 19 E3
Nilgala Cl EX39 18 C2
Norah Bellot Ct EX32 3 B3
Norfolk Ter EX39 12 D5
Normandy Ho EX32 3 D4
North Av EX39 19 H5
North Down Rd EX39 8 D2
North Grn EX32 13 E4
North La EX31 11 F5
North Rd,
 Barnstaple EX32 12 C2
North Rd,
 Bideford EX39 19 E4
North St,
 Bideford EX39 19 E4
North St,
 Braunton EX33 8 E2
North View Av EX39 18 D3
North View Hill EX39 18 D3
North Walk EX31 3 A3
Northam By-Pass
 EX39 17 D3
Northam Rd EX39 18 D2
Northcott Gdns EX39 17 F3
Northdene EX39 18 C2
Northdown Dr EX39 18 C4
Northdown Rd EX39 18 C4
Northfield La EX31 12 B2

Northfield Pk EX31 12 B1
Northfield Rd,
 Bideford EX39 19 G5
Northfield Rd,
 Ilfracombe EX34 4 B2
Nunnery Walk EX39 19 E5
Nursery End EX31 12 B2
Nuttaberry Hill EX39 19 F5
Oak Tree Dr EX32 13 H5
Oak Tree Gdns EX34 4 C2
Oakhill Rise EX31 11 G6
Oakland Av EX31 11 H5
Oakland Pk South
 EX31 11 G5
Oaklea Cres EX31 10 A6
Oakleigh Rd EX32 3 B2
Oakwell EX31 11 F5
Oakwell Cl EX38 20 E2
Oakwood Cl EX31 14 C1
Oatlands Av EX32 15 G2
Ocean Park App EX39 17 A3
Ochil Cl EX39 19 G6
Odun Rd EX39 16 B3
Old Barnstaple Rd
 EX34 5 E5
Old Barnstaple Rd,
 Bideford EX39 19 F4
Old Barnstaple Rd,
 Braunton EX33 8 F3
Old Barnstaple Rd,
 Ilfracombe EX34 4 D3
Old Berrynarbor Rd
 EX34 4 F2
Old Bideford Rd EX31 14 A1
Old Exeter Rd EX32 15 G3
Old Farm Ct EX31 12 B6
Old Quay La EX39 16 D3
Old Rectory Cl EX39 16 F1
Old School La EX31 10 B6
Old School Rd EX32 15 H1
Old Station Rd EX32 13 E5
Old Sticklepath Hill
 EX31 12 A5
Old Torrington Rd,
 Barnstaple EX32 12 A6
Old Torrington Rd,
 Roundswell EX31 14 B3
Old Town EX39 18 D5
Oliver Rd EX32 13 E3
One End St EX39 16 B2
Ora Cl EX33 7 C5
Ora La EX33 7 C5
Ora Stone Pk EX33 7 B6
Orange La EX39 16 B3
Orchard Cl,
 Barnstaple EX32 11 H6
Orchard Cl,
 Braunton EX33 8 C3
Orchard Cl,
 Combe Martin EX34 6 D2
Orchard Cotts EX32 14 C5
Orchard Gdns EX39 18 D2
Orchard Gro EX33 7 C5
Orchard Hill EX39 18 D2
Orchard Rd,
 Barnstaple EX32 12 D5
Orchard Rd,
 Braunton EX33 9 A1
Orchard Rise EX39 19 E2
Orchard Ter EX32 13 E3
Osborne Rd EX32 18 B4
Osborne La EX39 18 B4
Osborne Rd EX34 4 B2
Oswald Browning Way
 EX32 12 D2
Otter Way EX32 13 F5
Oxford Gro EX34 4 C2
Oxford Pk EX34 4 C2
Oxmans La EX39 17 E3
Paiges La EX31 3 B3
Palmers Cl EX33 8 D3
Palmers EX38 20 E2
Pannier Mkt EX38 20 D3
Park Av,
 Barnstaple EX31 11 H5
Park Av, Bideford EX39 19 E4
Park Av,
 Westward Ho EX39 17 B3
Park Cl EX31 10 B6
Park Cres EX34 6 D3
Park Ct EX34 4 C4
Park Hill Rd EX34 4 C3
Park La,
 Barnstaple EX32 12 D5
Park La, Bideford EX39 19 E3
Park La,
 Combe Martin EX34 6 C3
Park Ter EX32 3 D6
Park View Cl EX34 6 D3
Park View Rd EX32 3 C1
Park Villas,
 Barnstaple EX32 15 H5

Park Villas,
 Braunton EX33 8 D3
Park Vw EX31 12 B6
Park Way EX34 4 C4
Parkers Hollow EX31 11 G6
Parkes Rd EX38 20 F3
Parklands EX31 11 G6
Parkview Ter EX39 17 B3
Paternosta Row EX31 3 B4
Pathfield Cl EX31 11 F6
Pathfield Lawn EX31 3 A1
Pathfields,
 Braunton EX33 7 C4
Pathfields,
 Torrington EX38 20 F2
Pear Tree Way EX32 14 B5
Peards Down Cl EX32 13 G5
Pebbleridge Rd EX39 17 B3
Pentice La EX34 6 E2
Periwinkle Dr EX31 11 G6
Philip Av EX31 14 C1
Phillip Av EX31 12 A6
Pill Gdns EX33 8 D4
Pill La,
 Barnstaple EX32 15 F2
Pill La,
 Barnstaple EX32 15 G1
Pill Rd EX39 19 E4
Pilland Way EX31 11 H3
Pilton Causeway EX32 3 B2
Pilton Lawn EX32 3 C1
Pilton Quay EX31 3 A1
Pilton St EX31 3 B1
Pine Cl EX34 4 E3
Pitt Av EX39 16 B3
Pitt Hill EX39 16 A4
Pitt La EX39 19 E4
Pixie Dell EX33 8 B2
Pixie La EX33 8 B2
Poleshill La EX31 12 A1
Policemans Hill EX32 15 G4
Poltimore Lawn EX32 12 D3
Polywell EX39 16 A2
Poole La EX34 7 D2
Portland Pk EX34 4 D2
Portland St,
 Barnstaple EX32 12 D5
Portland St,
 Ilfracombe EX34 4 C2
Portmarsh La EX32 3 D6
Potacre St EX38 20 D2
Potterswell EX31 11 F6
Pottery La EX31 9 C5
Pottington Bsns Pk
 EX31 11 H2
Pottington Rd EX31 12 A3
Pottington Rd EX31 12 B3
Pound La EX34 6 E3
Poundfield Cl EX31 10 C6
Poundfld Cl EX31 10 C6
Poyers EX33 9 A1
Pretoria Ter EX34 4 B4
Prideaux Mdw EX38 20 F2
Primrose Av EX32 13 G4
Primrose La EX39 16 A4
Princess Av EX34 4 C2
Princess St EX32 3 C2
Priory Cl EX31 12 B2
Priory Gdns EX31 12 B2
Priory Rd EX31 12 C2
Promenade EX34 4 C1
Prospect Pl EX32 12 D6
Pulchrass St EX32 3 D4
Pusehill Rd EX39 17 A4
Pynes La EX39 18 C6
Pynes Walk EX39 18 C6
Quantocks EX33 8 B2
Quarry Cl EX39 18 C4
Quay La EX39 16 D2
Quayfield Path EX34 4 D2
Quayfield Rd EX34 4 D2
Quayside EX31 3 A4
Queen Annes Ct EX31 3 A4
Queen Annes Mws
 EX31 3 A4
Queen St,
 Barnstaple EX32 3 C4
Queen St,
 Bideford EX39 19 E4
Queens Av EX34 4 D3
Rack Park Cl EX38 20 C3
Rackfield Ct EX32 3 B2
Railway Ter EX39 19 F5
Raleigh Heights EX31 12 C2
Raleigh Hill EX39 18 B1
Raleigh Lawn EX31 12 C2
Raleigh Mdw EX32 12 D2
Raleigh Rd EX32 12 D2
Ralph Rd EX33 8 B2
Ravelin Gdns EX32 13 E4
Ravelin Manor Rd
 EX32 12 D4
Rectory Cl EX33 9 B1

Rectory La EX39 16 E1
Rectory Rd EX39 18 D4
Rectory Rd EX34 6 D4
Red La EX31 10 C5
Redlands Rd EX31 10 C5
Reform St EX31 3 B1
Regent Cl,
 Bickington EX31 11 H6
Regent Cl,
 Fremington EX31 10 C6
Regent Pl EX34 4 C2
Rews Cl EX34 6 C1
Rhododendron Av
 EX31 11 H5
Richard Cl EX39 18 C6
Richmond Av EX34 4 B3
Richmond Grn EX39 16 A3
Richmond Pk EX39 17 D3
Richmond Rd,
 Bideford EX39 16 A3
Richmond Rd,
 Ilfracombe EX34 4 B3
Richmond St EX32 3 D2
Richmond Walk EX32 3 D2
Riddell Av EX39 3 B1
Ridge Hill EX34 6 C4
Ridgeway Cl EX39 17 C3
Ridgeway Ct EX39 17 C3
Ridgeway Dr EX39 17 C3
Ridgwy Av EX39 17 C3
River Taw EX31 3 B4
Riversdale Av EX34 4 B2
Riverside Ct,
 Barnstaple EX32 3 A4
Riverside Ct,
 Bideford EX39 19 E2
Riverside Rd EX31 11 G2
Rivermeet EX39 16 A2
Robins Hill EX39 18 C2
Rock Av EX32 12 D6
Rock Gdns EX32 12 D5
Rock Hill EX33 8 C2
Rock La EX34 6 E3
Rockfield Rd EX34 7 A2
Rolle Ct EX38 20 C3
Rolle Quay EX31 3 A3
Rolle Rd EX38 20 C3
Rolle St EX31 3 A2
Rooks Cl EX31 11 G6
Rooks Farm Rd EX31 9 C5
Ropery Rd EX34 4 D2
Ropewalk EX39 19 E4
Rosalie Ter*,
 South St EX34 7 B3
Roscoff Cl EX38 20 E2
Rose La EX32 13 E5
Rosea Bridge La EX34 6 C2
Rosemoor Rd EX38 20 E2
Rosewood Gro EX31 11 H6
Roslyn Ter EX31 12 B3
Roundswell Bsns Pk
 EX31 14 B1
Roundswell
 Commercial Pk
 EX31 14 B1
Roundswell Ind Est
 EX31 14 C1
Roundswell Link Rd
 EX31 11 G6
Rowan Pk EX31 11 G6
Rows La EX34 6 E4
Royston Rd EX39 18 D5
Rumsam Cl EX32 15 G1
Rumsam Gdns EX32 15 H1
Rumsam Rd EX32 15 G1
Runnacleave Rd EX34 4 B2
Rupertswood Ter EX34 4 D2
Rushcott Cl EX31 9 B5
Russell Cl EX32 14 C6
Sage Park Rd EX33 8 B1
St Bannocks Park Rd
 EX34 4 C3
St Brannocks Hill EX33 8 D2
St Brannocks Rd EX34 4 B3
St Brannocks Well Cl
 EX33 8 D1
St Catherines Cl EX31 9 B5
St Georges Rd EX32 3 B1
St Helens Cl EX33 7 C6
St James Cl EX32 14 C6
St James Pl EX34 4 C1
St Johns La EX32 13 E6
St Keyes Cl EX32 14 B5
St Margarets Gdn EX31 3 A1
St Marys Cl EX32 20 B4
St Marys Rd,
 Barnstaple EX32 3 D2
St Marys Rd,
 Braunton EX33 7 C5
St Peters Rd EX32 10 B5
St Peters Ter EX34 4 C2
St Teresas Ct EX39 17 D3
Salem Sq EX32 3 C5

Street	Postcode	Grid
Salem St	EX32	3 C5
Salt Wood La	EX34	6 B2
Saltmer Cl	EX34	5 B5
Sanctuary Cl	EX32	15 H4
Sanders La	EX32	15 G4
Sandfords Gdns	EX38	20 D3
Sandpiper Ct	EX34	7 D2
Sandy La, Croyde	EX33	7 B5
Sandy La, Woolacombe	EX34	7 B2
Sandy Way	EX33	7 C2
Sandymere Rd	EX39	17 D2
Saunton Cl	EX33	8 C2
Saunton Rd	EX33	8 A1
Saxons Cft	EX32	13 F6
School Cl	EX31	10 B5
School La, Barnstaple	EX32	15 G4
School La, Torrington	EX38	20 C2
Score Vw	EX34	4 C4
Scott Av	EX39	16 A2
Scurfield	EX33	8 D2
Scurfield Cl	EX33	8 D2
Sea View Rd	EX39	17 E3
Searle Ter	EX39	17 F4
Seaside	EX34	6 B1
Second Field La	EX33	8 C3
Sentry Cnr	EX39	14 F5
Sentry La	EX32	15 G4
Seven Acre La	EX33	8 E3
Seven Acre Pk	EX33	8 E3
Seven Brethren Bank	EX31	3 B5
Shackhayes	EX34	6 C2
Shaftesbury Rd	EX34	4 D2
Shame Face La	EX31	12 A2
Sharlands La	EX33	8 C2
Shearford La	EX33	12 C1
Sherratts Oak	EX32	12 D2
Shieling Rd	EX31	11 E5
Shore Ct	EX34	6 B2
Shoreland Way	EX39	17 E3
Shorelands Rd	EX31	12 A6
Shorelands Way	EX31	12 A6
Short Cl	EX39	18 B4
Shortacombe Dr	EX33	8 A1
Shrubbery Cl	EX32	13 E6
Shute La	EX34	6 D2
Signal Ter	EX31	3 A5
Silford Rd	EX39	18 B1
Silvan Dr	EX33	8 D2
Silver Birch Ct	EX31	11 H6
Silver St, Appledore	EX39	16 B2
Silver St, Barnstaple	EX32	3 C4
Silver St, Bideford	EX39	19 E5
Silver St, Braunton	EX33	8 D1
Silverwood Heights	EX32	13 E2
Sings La	EX33	8 D3
Skern Cl	EX39	17 E2
Skern Way	EX39	17 E2
Skirhead La	EX34	6 F4
Skylark Spinney	EX31	14 A1
Slade Rd, Bideford	EX39	18 C4
Slade Rd, Ilfracombe	EX34	4 B4
Slade Valley Rd	EX34	4 B4
Sloe La	EX32	14 B5
Smoky House La	EX31	13 E1
Soloman Dr	EX39	19 E6
Somerset Pl	EX32	3 C4
Something La	EX33	7 C6
Sommers Cres	EX34	4 C2
South Av	EX39	19 G5
South Bank Dr	EX39	18 D4
South Burrow Rd	EX34	4 B3
South Dr	EX38	20 D3
South Grn	EX32	13 E5
South Hayes	EX32	14 B5
South Hayes Copse	EX32	14 C5
South Pk, Barnstaple	EX32	12 D6
South Pk, Braunton	EX33	8 E3
South Rd	EX39	16 B3
South St, Barnstaple	EX32	12 D6
South St, Braunton	EX33	8 D4
South St, Torrington	EX38	20 D3
South St, Woolacombe	EX34	7 B3
South View Cl	EX33	8 D4
South Vw, Barnstaple	EX31	12 A2
South Vw, Ilfracombe	EX34	4 A3
South Walk	EX32	3 C6
Southcott Rd	EX39	18 D3
Southfield Rd	EX39	19 G5
Southlands, Braunton	EX33	8 D3
Southlands, Wrafton	EX33	9 A1
Southlea, Bideford	EX39	17 D4
Southlea, Braunton	EX33	8 E3
Southlea Cl	EX33	8 E3
Southwood Dr	EX39	18 D3
Sowden La	EX32	12 D4
Sowden Pk	EX32	13 F5
Speedwell Cl	EX32	13 G5
Spring Cl	EX39	17 D4
Springfield Av	EX32	12 D6
Springfield Cres, Barnstaple	EX31	10 C5
Springfield Cres, Bideford	EX39	17 E3
Springfield Rd, Barnstaple	EX31	11 G6
Springfield Rd, Ilfracombe	EX34	4 C2
Springfield Rd, Woolacombe	EX34	7 B2
Springfield Ter, Bideford	EX39	19 F5
Springfield Ter, Westward Ho	EX39	17 B3
Spurway Gdns	EX34	6 E4
Staddon Cl	EX33	8 C2
Staddon Rd	EX39	16 A3
Staggers La	EX31	9 B2
Stallards	EX33	8 C2
Stanbridge Pk	EX39	18 B4
Stanbury Copse	EX34	4 B3
Stanwell Dr	EX39	17 B4
Stanwell Hill	EX39	17 A4
Station Cl	EX33	8 D3
Station Rd, Barnstaple	EX31	3 A6
Station Rd, Braunton	EX33	8 D3
Station Rd, Ilfracombe	EX34	4 B3
Station Rd, Woolacombe	EX34	7 D3
Stella Maris Ct	EX39	19 E4
Stentaway La	EX33	7 C4
Sticklepath Ct	EX31	12 B5
Sticklepath Hill	EX31	12 A5
Sticklepath Ter	EX31	12 B5
Stoat Pk	EX33	13 F5
Stonemans La	EX38	20 C2
Stoneywell	EX39	16 D2
Stony La	EX39	16 A3
Strand Ct	EX39	19 E4
Stucley Rd	EX39	18 C6
Style Cl	EX32	15 G1
Summerland St	EX32	3 C4
Sunflower Rd	EX32	3 D3
Sunny Bank	EX32	12 D4
Sunny Ct	EX34	7 B2
Sunnyside, Bideford	EX39	19 F5
Sunnyside, Combe Martin	EX34	6 E3
Sunnyside Rd	EX34	4 A2
Sunset Heights	EX32	3 D3
Sunset Mws	EX32	12 D4
Swallow Cl	EX32	13 H4
Swallow Fld	EX31	11 F6
Swanswood Gdns	EX39	17 B3
Tadworthy Rd	EX39	17 D3
Tamar Rd	EX31	9 D3
Tanners La	EX32	14 B4
Tarry La	EX34	4 C2
Taw Cl	EX32	3 C5
Taw Meadow Cres	EX31	10 C5
Taw Rd	EX31	9 D5
Taw Vale	EX32	3 C5
Taw Vw	EX31	10 C5
Tennacott Heights	EX39	19 G6
Tennacott La	EX39	19 H6
Tews La	EX31	11 F5
Tewsley Cl	EX31	11 F5
The Brittons	EX33	8 D3
The Coombes	EX31	11 F6
The Copse	EX31	11 F6
The Esplanade	EX34	7 A2
The Fairway	EX33	8 A2
The Fairways	EX39	17 C3
The Grange	EX33	8 E3
The Green	EX31	10 A5
The Hermitage	EX34	4 B2
The Hollies	EX31	11 G6
The Lanes	EX34	4 C2
The Laurels	EX31	14 B1
The Lees	EX34	5 B5
The Links	EX39	17 D3
The Moorings	EX33	8 D2
The Mount	EX39	16 A2
The Orchard	EX31	11 F5
The Orchards	EX32	14 B5
The Path	EX39	16 B1
The Pollards	EX32	13 F6
The Quay, Appledore	EX39	16 B2
The Quay, Bideford	EX39	19 E4
The Quay, Ilfracombe	EX34	4 D1
The Rock	EX31	12 C2
The Shields, Ilfracombe	EX34	4 D3
The Shields, Ilfracombe	EX34	4 C3
The Square, Barnstaple	EX32	3 B4
The Square, Bideford	EX39	17 E3
The Square, Bishops Tawton	EX32	15 G4
The Square, Braunton	EX33	8 D2
The Strand, Barnstaple	EX31	3 B4
The Strand, Bideford	EX39	19 E4
The Willows	EX31	10 C5
Theatre La	EX31	3 B4
Thornlea Av	EX31	10 A6
Tom Sanders Cl	EX34	6 D3
Tomouth Cres	EX39	16 B3
Tomouth Rd	EX39	16 B3
Torridge Bri	EX39	19 E2
Torridge Cl	EX39	19 F5
Torridge Hill	EX39	19 E5
Torridge Mt	EX39	19 F5
Torridge Pl	EX39	19 E5
Torridge Rd, Barnstaple	EX31	9 C3
Torridge Rd, Bideford	EX39	16 A2
Torridge Vw	EX38	20 B2
Torrington La	EX39	19 F5
Torrington St	EX39	19 F5
Torrs Pk	EX34	4 A3
Torrs Walk Av	EX34	4 B2
Tower St*, Butt Gdn St	EX39	19 E5
Town Farm Ct	EX33	8 C2
Town Pk	EX38	20 C2
Town Walk	EX32	12 D5
Towns End	EX33	8 C2
Trafalgar Lawn	EX32	12 D5
Treefield Walk	EX32	13 G5
Trenode Av	EX34	6 C2
Trent Cl	EX39	19 H6
Trinity Gdns	EX34	4 B3
Trinity Pl	EX32	3 C5
Trinity St	EX32	3 C4
Trouville Calvados	EX32	3 D4
Tudor Cl	EX34	17 E4
Tudor Dr	EX31	11 H6
Tuly St	EX31	3 A3
Two Rivers Ind Est	EX31	11 H2
Two Trees Rd	EX31	10 B6
Umber Cl	EX34	6 C2
Umberside	EX34	6 E3
Under Minnow Rd	EX31	11 E2
Union Cl	EX39	18 D5
Upcott Av	EX31	11 H2
Upcott Hill	EX39	19 E6
Upper Torrs Pk	EX34	4 A3
Upton Rd	EX39	19 F5
Usticke La	EX34	6 F3
Vale Cl	EX32	3 D1
Valley Cl	EX32	13 E3
Valley La	EX34	6 D2
Valley Vw, Barnstaple	EX32	14 C6
Valley Vw, Bideford	EX39	18 B4
Velator Cl	EX33	8 D4
Velator Dr	EX33	8 D4
Velator Lane Av	EX33	8 D3
Velator Rd	EX33	8 D4
Vellator Ind Est	EX33	8 D4
Vellator Way	EX33	8 D4
Venlock Cl	EX32	13 G5
Venn Cl	EX39	16 F1
Venn Rd	EX32	15 H1
Venton Dr	EX39	17 B3
Vernons La	EX39	16 B2
Vicarage Lawn	EX32	3 C3
Vicarage Rd	EX32	14 A5
Vicarage St	EX32	3 B3
Vickers Grnd	EX39	17 E2
Victoria Cl	EX32	12 D5
Victoria Gdns	EX39	19 E5
Victoria Gro	EX39	19 E5
Victoria Lawn	EX32	12 D5
Victoria Rd, Barnstaple	EX32	12 D5
Victoria Rd, Ilfracombe	EX34	4 C2
Victoria St, Barnstaple	EX32	12 D5
Victoria St, Combe Martin	EX34	6 E4
Victoria Ter	EX32	3 D6
Villa Cl	EX32	15 H1
Villa Rd	EX38	20 C3
Village Cotts	EX32	15 G4
Village St	EX32	15 G4
Virginia Cl	EX39	18 D6
Wakeham Ct	EX33	8 D3
Walnut Way	EX32	13 F5
Walton Way	EX32	13 E4
Warfield Villas	EX34	4 D2
Warren Cl	EX34	20 B2
Warren La	EX38	20 B2
Warren Vw	EX39	18 C4
Water La, Barnstaple	EX32	12 D6
Water La, Combe Martin	EX34	6 D3
Water Lane Cl	EX32	12 D6
Water Park Rd	EX39	18 B4
Water Ter	EX34	6 D3
Waterloo Ter	EX39	18 C5
Watermouth Rd	EX34	4 E2
Watery La, Braunton	EX33	8 F3
Watery La, Combe Martin	EX34	6 E3
Watery La, Croyde	EX33	7 C5
Watery La, Taddiport	EX38	20 B3
Watery La, Torrington	EX38	20 E2
Wayfaring	EX32	13 F6
Weirside Way	EX32	12 D2
Welch's La	EX31	9 A6
Weld Park Rd	EX34	4 E2
Well Park Rd	EX39	20 D3
Well St	EX38	20 D3
Wellclose Rd	EX33	8 D3
Wells St	EX32	3 B4
West Av	EX31	12 A5
West Challacombe La	EX34	6 C2
West Cross	EX33	8 C2
West Croyde	EX33	7 B6
West Hill La	EX33	8 C2
West Meadow Cl	EX33	8 A1
West Meadow Rd	EX33	8 A2
West Moor	EX39	17 E2
West Moor Cl	EX39	17 E2
West Moor Way	EX39	17 E2
West Pk	EX33	8 C3
West Rd	EX34	7 B3
West Ter	EX38	20 B2
West View Av	EX39	19 F4
West Yelland	EX31	9 A6
Westacott Mdw	EX32	13 H5
Westacott Rd	EX32	13 G5
Westaway	EX31	1
Westaway Cl	EX31	1
Westaway Plain	EX31	1
Westborne Gro	EX34	
Westbourne Ter	EX39	1
Westcombe La	EX39	1
Wester Moor Cl	EX31	1
Wester Moor Dr	EX31	1
Wester Moor Way	EX31	1
Western Av	EX39	1
Western Gdns	EX34	1
Western Rise	EX34	
Western Ter	EX34	
Westfield Av	EX31	1
Westlands	EX33	
Westmead Cl	EX33	
Westminster Villas	EX34	
Wet La	EX34	
Whiddon Dr	EX32	1
Whiddon Valley Ind Est		1
White Gates	EX34	
White House Cl	EX34	1
Whitehorse La	EX39	
Whitemoor Hill	EX32	1
Whiteridge Pl	EX34	
Whites La, Barnstaple	EX32	1
Whites La, Torrington	EX38	2
Whittingham Rd	EX34	
Wilder Rd	EX34	
Wilkey Cl	EX34	1
Willand Rd	EX33	
Willet St	EX39	1
Williams Cl	EX33	
Willow Cl	EX34	
Willow Gro	EX39	1
Willow Tree Rd	EX32	1
Willoway Cl	EX33	
Willoway Gro	EX33	
Willoway La	EX33	
Willowfield Cl	EX33	
Willshere Rd	EX32	
Windmill La	EX39	1
Windsor Ct	EX34	
Windsor Rd, Barnstaple	EX32	
Windsor Rd, Bideford	EX39	
Windy Ash Hill	EX32	1
Windy Cross	EX38	2
Withywell La	EX33	
Wood La	EX34	
Wooda Rd	EX39	1
Woodland Cl	EX32	1
Woodland Pk	EX39	1
Woodland Vw	EX31	
Woodlands	EX34	
Woodlark La	EX31	
Woodville Cl	EX31	
Woolacombe Ct	EX34	
Woolacombe Rise	EX34	
Woolbarn Lawn	EX32	1
Wordsworth Av	EX31	1
Worlington Hill	EX39	1
Worth Rd	EX34	
Wrafton Rd	EX33	
Wren Cl	EX31	
Wrey Av	EX31	
Wyndthorpe Gdns	EX34	
Yellaford Way	EX31	1
Yelland Rd	EX31	
Yellaton La	EX34	
Yeo Dr	EX39	1
Yeo Rd	EX31	
Yeo Vale Rd	EX32	
Youings Dr	EX31	
Youngaton Rd	EX31	1
Zephyr Cres	EX32	1
Zions Pl	EX32	

Edition 563 D 05...